AF199132

DIANA'S DARKEST DIARY

number two

from an author, a poetess
broken by life

not allowed to escape
the way i want to
so here is where i escape
i'm sorry if you can relate

and all sudden nothing matters anymore, she said

*"we feel connection to where
a presence still might be.
we will now carry on a life for
those who cannot
see."*

-devilskin, in black

what i'm doing for the person i lost long ago
rest in peace

and all sudden nothing matters anymore, she said

the poetry i write

is deeper

than my cuts

but they stop bleeding

and all sudden nothing matters anymore, she said

-diana's darkest diary — the second — 2018-

when i was nine years old i
rode my mountain bike
up the highest mountains
on top i was so freaking proud
i smiled and then i
hurried down
at tempo limit seventy
i hit the same
then life hit me

i could have hurt myself when falling off
my bike
even though i wasn't careful
i never did
i always caused

pain but never

accidentally

and all sudden nothing matters anymore, she said

the last years i spent my
winters and beginnings of
spring

in psychiatry

then this year
arrived
and taught me

it's not seasonal
no month is

mild
towards my struggle

the sun won't save my brain

and all sudden nothing matters anymore, she said

-diana's **darkest diary** – the second – 2018-

emetophobia **made** me become scared
of my **body**

but my **body should** better be

scared

of

m e

she **told me**

-lesson **learned**

and all **sudden nothing** matters anymore, she said

-diana's darkest diary – the second – 2018-

meeting new people makes me
start to hate
them
new situations scare me
and i get up becoming
the center of attention
making them love me
hate me
don't care

but they are new i
want to
cut their
lives
at first

if i get over me
i'll be your best friend
or your worst enemy
accept the end

we're temporary

BUTDON'TLOOKATME IF YOU DON'T WANNA STAY

FOREVER

scares me

let me go

-diana 1 against diana 2

and all sudden nothing matters anymore, she said

i'm changing constantly
i'm never satisfied with something
for a longer

while

finding old pictures of

me

what a pretty girl
i hope she knows

she's me but
i cannot see

myself

in her

or any mirror

there are hundreds of me

and they're all

crazy

and all sudden nothing matters anymore, she said

-diana's darkest diary — the second — 2018-

i was called a psycho
by bullies
and my parents
sometimes they were the
same

i always yelled 'i'm not'
being convinced it was awful
to be

unusual

or even sick

but hey i'm a psycho
and i'll accept it

i need accept my illnesses
before trying to make them

leave

it's not that easy

-step one: 2015

 step two: as far away as pluto

and all sudden nothing matters anymore, she said

i fill my wardrobe with
clothes
i'm unsure about
to
fill the

emptiness inside
of me
leaving my stomach empty

because of it

not because i must
just because i can't
i'm not worth it

and all sudden nothing matters anymore, she said

i'm as paradox as

the girl who jumps down a tower

wanting to fly

but knowing

she'll die

oh

and all sudden nothing matters anymore, she said

-diana's darkest diary – the second – 2018-

imagine my mind as a chessboard
all black and white

and always different but

there are no rules

just rulers

and all sudden nothing matters anymore, she said

find the mistake
my dear

sleeping suicidal days away
doesn't work for
me
due to the nightmares
that weaken me
make me need to
recover
from time
that should have given
me
energy

were you successful?
did you
find it?

no?
see

there's no mistake

the mistake

is me

and all sudden nothing matters anymore, she said

my eating is so disordered
that supermarkets scare me
some days
and hunger is unknown
i just know pain
i lost 26 pounds
and got them back

i don't remember anything

i love my body

but i hate my mind

-fuck you

and all sudden nothing matters anymore, she said

my head seems to hurt a lot
since I was a
little child
maybe because
the pain inside my
brain
was too much for me then

then it became better to handle
and now
it starts again

-back at it

and all sudden nothing matters anymore, she said

i was too done
my body was drained
by my psyche
by my
thoughts of suicide
thoughts of giving in
wishing I never met
anyone
then you saw me
don't know why but
there's this energy
you keep
you gave to me
my head shut up for a
while
as we sit outside
three human beings
fucked by life
you held me
singing a song i wrote
talking about how much
i make them want to
keep going
and what my projects mean
to them
calling me by my
right name
what should i say
giving it back

i don't deserve you

and all sudden nothing matters anymore, she said

i want to go home
the place i live in
isn't
my trouble was born
here
and I can't let
it die
where they give its
flower poisonous water

without being sorry
but hey, you love
me
you say
if you love me

let me go
somewhere i can
h e a l

and all sudden nothing matters anymore, she said

-diana's darkest diary – the second – 2018-

in my nightmares
there are
awful animals
mad monsters
deadly demons
howling
the
deadname
eating the peace i'm
trying to
find

they're human

-when i slept at school and was glad that nobody had to
see me waking up in horror, 14112018

and all sudden nothing matters anymore, she said

-diana's darkest diary – the second – 2018-

i'm clearly addicted
to certain things
i don't want to
talk about by
now you might
become skeptical about
the person you
know the person
that i am

and all sudden nothing matters anymore, she said

i'm too much

i'm the one that
needs therapy twice a week
with a therapist
gives up on her
free time
to talk longer to me
than she's payed for

i'm the one that
the teachers need to
take care of
i can't speak up
read out loud
do every task and
i need more
time

they say i'm so quiet
it's because the voices
inside of me
are
so much louder

i'm louder as they shut themselves up
choke each other so
serotonin can visit me
hello stranger
or when they
win

run
i'm getting dangerous

and all sudden nothing matters anymore, she said

the feeling of
suffer
physical weakness
a numb body
a frozen brain
and eyes that never
seem to close
is the worst
but
i experienced too many
emotions i all considered
to be the
worst
can't decide about them
by now

-dear medication, why aren't you reliable?

and all sudden nothing matters anymore, she said

-diana's darkest diary – the second – 2018-

people think they can
provoke
hurt
bully
destroy
a single human soul
and judge it later
for being broken
having no empathy
being shocked
when
it
explodes

one cannot hold this in
forever

right now, it's him

two years ago
it would have been

m e

-i wanted to kill them. i didn't

and all sudden nothing matters anymore, she said

his
empty eyes
cut me like
a blade that
was kissed by
the devil
cut his
tongue through
and swallowed
the blood
of his
lambs of licorice
mixed with his
own
they deserved freedom
but were served on
the plate
of god

who's worth a living?
nobody should die for anyone

he deserves a better life, man

and all sudden nothing matters anymore, she said

she cares about those broken souls
recognizes them by
a crawling connection that
makes her want to
love their shattered pieces
make them whole

years ago, she would have needed someone
like herself

and all sudden nothing matters anymore, she said

i wonder what the mind
of a healthy
person
is like
they do not understand me
i wouldn't understand them
either

i guess

and all sudden nothing matters anymore, she said

she's an odd beauty
living at the dark side
of the moon
i'm a pretty nightmare
at the light one
dancing among the craters
feeling lighter
than ever
and as i waft through the
non-existent atmosphere
i hope
she's on the way, too
let's meet in the middle
between shadow and light
and forever will be

promised

and all sudden nothing matters anymore, she said

i don't control my emotions
my emotions
take all
control
of
me

everything is too much
and sometimes
you don't even want to
understand

and all sudden nothing matters anymore, she said

they're always shocked
as i pull out my
laptop
because it's
damaged
dirty
wrecked
but to me
it's pretty
pretty usual
must be similar
with my head

i wear it on my wrists
and they're alarmed
i can't see it

they wouldn't survive
with my considerations

and all sudden nothing matters anymore, she said

a gun
might kill dozens of
people
but
a word is a weapon
destructively
but
spread of silence
in the worst moments
causes death
itself
actually, guns do not murder
neither do words
or silence
it's all about humans
we're parasites

and all sudden nothing matters anymore, she said

-diana's **darkest diary** – the second – 2018-

red does **fade to rose**
rose **does fade to** white

don't **leave me please**
or leave **my brain**

-it won't

and all **sudden nothing** matters anymore, she said

-diana's darkest diary — the second — 2018-

i'm always late
but i matured too early
what if time is a lie
we all torture ourselves
through a concept
that can't even be
real

and all sudden nothing matters anymore, she said

philosophes argue about the
question of freedom
in my opinion
we're not born free
we're born into a
system we need to
keep together
and even are judged if we
try to

escape

and all sudden nothing matters anymore, she said

anxiety and depression do not
go together in a
good way
i always disappoint one of
them
but no matter who i give in
to
i'm always a disappointment
to
the person of mine

and all sudden nothing matters anymore, she said

-diana's darkest diary – the second – 2018-

i'd
say that
my brain
hates me
but it
lets me
write a
lot of
poetry

it loves me, i guess
i wish, i could love it
back

-always fighting against myself

and all sudden nothing matters anymore, she said

my body craves the pain
i told a friend
no, she said
it would be about my
mind because my body
always tries to heal
me no matter how
awful i treat it

my mind is my dictator
and i'm the enemy

and all sudden nothing matters anymore, she said

-diana's darkest diary — the second — 2018-

i always try my best
on stage
it's like home to me
my heart says yes but
my anxiety
says
no
and my body loses
control
and i speak shaking
trembling
feeling sick

but i speak
and i sing
cause i got talent
mental illness better not eat it up

-being on stage is always special to me

and all sudden nothing matters anymore, she said

-diana's darkest diary — the second — 2018-

i wish i knew if
my sadism is actually
just a kink
or connected to my
anger issues

-diana 2 is a masochist

and all sudden nothing matters anymore, she said

sometimes i'm glad
most of my closest
friends are fucked up
too
they disagree with my
behavior when it's toxic
but they
understand
because my psyche
is not about common sense

it's completely messed up
and horrifying

most of them tell me,
they know they're sick
as well
but when i tell them
about my brain they
tell me
they wouldn't survive
with a mind like mine

-my biggest achievement is staying alive

and all sudden nothing matters anymore, she said

i'm told i shouldn't
hurt myself but when
i hurt others instead i'm
told to stop so i destroy
belongings of mine or
others and if this happens
i also should prevent myself
from doing so as i scream it
out i'm just told to
quit

i can't
i'm impulsive, aggressive
and i never learned how to
deal with it

it's your fault, my dear

and all sudden nothing matters anymore, she said

and suddenly
psychiatry
started to feel like
home
i was not confused
about it
the others were

and all sudden nothing matters anymore, she said

i wanted to end my life
not to end my pain
just because i never saw
a reason to stay
when i become suicidal
by now
it's really about ending my
pain
maybe i got understandable
now but before
i saw what "healthies" do
not see
is there a reason for everyone
to stay
or do we need to find it
ourselves?

somehow i'm glad i'm still here

and all sudden nothing matters anymore, she said

-diana's darkest diary – the second – 2018-

i'm still learning that
staying with someone
is about searching for
adventure in them
instead of thinking
it only can be found
in strangers
who crave me
i'd crave them too

but i'm mature enough
to say no
now

and all sudden nothing matters anymore, she said

mental breakdowns are
the capital of my
destiny of my
destruction
they're something like
what eating is for
them
a part of every day
and sometimes

too much

and all sudden nothing matters anymore, she said

every day is a battle
the weekdays do not matter
my heart's about to shatter
and free days won't save me
actually, they open up the
bottle of emptiness
but right now, i'm already
lost in it
and i feel like nothing can
take it away
i might manage to make
it through the
responsibilities but
i'm either living for work
or do nothing
at all

-i used to live for school for years

and all sudden nothing matters anymore, she said

i'm in highest heaven
or at the lowest level
my fire can die just as
fast as a candle
the grey in between
is too unclear to
handle

and all sudden nothing matters anymore, she said

-diana's darkest diary – the second – 2018-

i take medication to sleep
i take medication to make it
through the day
and i'm still barely functioning

am i really meant to be alive?

and all sudden nothing matters anymore, she said

i experienced lots of pain
in my early teen years
my worst heartbreaks
addictions
suicides
from age nine to fourteen
i cried the most tears
and now my heart seemed
to froze over
there are no tears left
to cry anymore
and my mouth is shut down
i'm sixteen
learning how to feel again
but i don't want this back
but on my numbest days
i even miss
the heartbreak

and all sudden nothing matters anymore, she said

-diana's darkest diary – the second – 2018-

it's like swimming in the
dangerous ocean never knowing
when a shark might appear
or the current takes me
with it and i'll be losing
track not knowing
what to do
against it
every day there is a new risk
i need to swim away from
but i'm not a professional
swimmer and i let it take
me and drown for a while
when it's done i must
try to take the rest of
the strength i own
swim to a lost island and stay
before the next day
leaves me in the waters
again

-the circle of the war inside of me

and all sudden nothing matters anymore, she said

she lives in my heart
deep inside of me
never alone
they both spend their
days to
hold it together
so i can make it through
the day
it helps me but it's
dangerous
if i lost them
i'd be lost
too

-i'm clearly addicted

and all sudden nothing matters anymore, she said

-diana's darkest diary — the second — 2018-

i'm asked if i am
scared
of myself
all i can say is

yes

of course

hella

sadly
you'd fear me, too

and all sudden nothing matters anymore, she said

i'm a broken wanderer
lost in the middle of lust
will i deny my desire
and run away
to fix myself?
let my holy harbor decide
my inner ship will never be wrong

and all sudden nothing matters anymore, she said

-diana's darkest diary – the second – 2018-

we'll be sitting
in class
educational
studies philosophy
whatever
they talk about these
things
being like
we all never experienced
this
"but imagine!!!"

.

.

.

you fucking
ignorant
liars

-living with several mental illnesses be like

and all sudden nothing matters anymore, she said

my personality is made
of tiny little fragments
from the others
from those around me
i'm an puzzle
always incomplete

but writing has always been
mine

and all sudden nothing matters anymore, she said

i do fake emotions
i wish I could experience

again

and all **sudden nothing** matters anymore, she said

people
are
i am poisonous to them
to you it's something different
me
life is physically painful
is
an
the illusion is me

and all sudden nothing matters anymore, she said

-diana's darkest diary — the second — 2018-

thanks a lot for buying this shattered piece of art

my cover is done by the beautiful @vivianvaia

a huge "thank you" to my friends,
who are always there to save me from myself
who take care of me
keep me warm and who are irreplaceable
i love you lots

i'm still struggling
i'm still fighting

i keep doing
i keep writing

and as long as i do write

my heart still feels hope
sparks of recovery shine brighter
than my past ever will

you'll see them, too

love,

madison diana

and all sudden nothing matters anymore, she said

-diana's darkest diary – the second – 2018-

Die Deutsche Nationalbibliothek verzeichnet diese Publikation in der Deutschen Nationalbibliografie; detaillierte bibliografische Daten sind im Internet über dnb.dnb.de abrufbar.

Herstellung und Verlag: BoD – Books on Demand, Norderstedt

and all sudden nothing matters anymore, she said

Herstellung und Verlag:

BoD – Books on Demand, Norderstedt

Bibliografische Information der Deutschen Nationalbibliothek

Die Deutsche Nationalbibliothek verzeichnet diese Publikation
in der Deutschen Nationalbibliografie; detaillierte bibliografische
Daten sind im Internet über http://dnb.d-nb.de abrufbar.

ISBN: 978-3-7481-2162-6